Reaching Tidewater

• *Life on the Delaware Canal* •

By
Noreen F. Moore

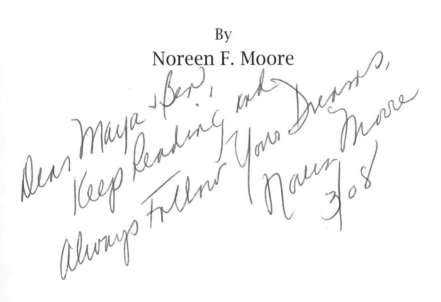

WHITE MANE KIDS
SHIPPENSBURG, PENNSYLVANIA

This White Mane Books publication
was printed by
Beidel Printing House, Inc.
63 West Burd Street
Shippensburg, PA 17257-0708 USA

The acid-free paper used in this book meets the guidelines for permanence and durability of the Committee on Production Guidelines for Book Longevity of the Council on Library Resources.

For a complete list of available publications
please write
White Mane Books
Division of White Mane Publishing Company, Inc.
P.O. Box 708
Shippensburg, PA 17257-0708 USA

Library of Congress Cataloging-in-Publication Data

Moore, Noreen F., 1961-
    Reaching tidewater : life on the Delaware Canal / by Noreen F. Moore.
        p. cm.
    Summary: In 1862, as the Civil War tears some families apart, twelve-year-old Anna joins her entire family--and even helps drive the mules--on a journey down the Delaware Canal, hauling a load of coal from Easton to Bristol, Pennsylvania.
    Includes bibliographical references.
    ISBN 1-57249-358-5 (alk. paper)
    1. Delaware Canal (Pa.)--Juvenile fiction. 2. Pennsylvania--History--Civil War, 1861-1865--Juvenile fiction. [1. Delaware Canal (Pa.)--Fiction. 2. Boats and boating--Fiction. 3. Family life--Pennsylvania--Fiction. 4. Pennsylvania--History--Civil War, 1861-1865--Fiction.] I. Title.

PZ7.M78745Re 2004
[Fic]--dc22

                                                                2004041935

For Bob, Meghan, Bobby, and Kaitlyn
and for my parents
who taught me that all I want to be
is within my reach.

Contents

Chapter One
• *Spring of 1862* •

Long before the sun rose in the sky, long before the crows even thought about crowing, I swung my legs out from under the covers and over the edge of my bed. My day had begun—it was four o'clock.

My job was to take care of the mules that towed the boat my father drove down the Delaware Canal. The lantern lit the path to the stable where Daisy and Belle waited patiently for their first meal of the day. It was mid-April and the morning mist and chill reminded me that it was early spring.

Mama and Daddy were in the kitchen gathering last-minute supplies for the first trip of the season down the Delaware Canal. My older brother John was in the stable preparing the feed baskets for the mules.

I picked up the brush and began gliding my hand along Daisy's shoulder and down her back. I had braided her mane and intertwined bright red yarn through her coarse hair days before. John said it looked silly. "She's a mule, Anna, not a doll," he said as he gathered the feed.

John had just turned sixteen, so he thought he knew everything, and I had to admit that he knew a lot more than I did. We worked by the light of the lantern that hung on a hook in the corner of the stable. John harnessed the mules after I brushed them and prepared them for their first day on the canal.

Daddy was a steersman, or a pilot, on a canal boat on the Delaware Canal. The Lehigh Coal & Navigation Company owned the boat and the numbers 526 were painted on its side. These numbers helped identify the boat.

Daddy always said, "Anna, you have the most important job, taking care of the mules. Without the mules the boat won't move and we won't eat." John had worked with Daddy on the canal for six years, and he wanted to move to the big city of Easton, but didn't tell Mama because she would always get upset when he talked about moving. Daddy loved the canal almost as much as he loved Mama.

We lived in the village of Smithtown, Pennsylvania, along the bank of the Delaware River. Mama loved Smithtown. The daughter of Irish immigrants who helped build the canal, she often talked about how hard her father and brothers had worked to build this great canal so that others like Daddy and John could make a good living and provide for their family. Mama was proud of her heritage and couldn't understand why John didn't feel the same and wanted to abandon family tradition and move to the big city.

Smithtown was a pleasant village. Our house was Mama's pride and joy, and the boat was Daddy's. Our house wasn't real big and the rooms were pretty small, but it was home. In our kitchen Mama prepared meals for our family of seven. In the middle of the room sat a large wooden table around which we gathered to nourish our stomachs and our hearts. Daddy and John told stories of canal trips often at this table.

John was the oldest at sixteen, and I was twelve. My sister Elizabeth was ten, our brother James eight, and George was four years old. The boys all shared one bedroom and Elizabeth and I shared another.

The kitchen was always the busiest room in the house; Mama prepared delicious meals and was often baking breads and cakes for Daddy and John to take on their trips down the Delaware Canal. During canning season we spent hours preserving fruits and vegetables so that we could enjoy them over the long, cold winter months.

My chores included taking care of the mules and helping Mama take care of my younger sister and brothers. Elizabeth, James, and George also had chores to do. They had to take care of and feed the goats and chickens. Mama often told them that they had the most important jobs because if we didn't keep the animals happy they wouldn't give us any milk or eggs. Mama also took great pride in her vegetable garden, even though the soil was filled with stones and was very hard. Every season she would perform miracles and encourage beautiful and delicious vegetables to grow.

Daddy always said that Smithtown was the best place to raise a family, especially a family in the canal boat business like ours. There were boat yards in nearby Erwinna and Uhlertown where boats could be repaired when needed, and shops for Mama to visit when she needed to order material for our dresses.

Daddy worked hard to give us the things he said we needed and should have. His trips on the canal began around four in the morning, after I had brushed, fed and harnessed the mules. On the canal, the days often ended around ten at night. The reason I know the days were that long is because John always complained about the long days and the little pay.

He was convinced that he could make more money in the big city working half as many hours as Daddy and he worked on the canal.

"Foolishness," Mama would always declare.

The lantern continued to illuminate the stable on that dark, damp April morning. I carefully lifted the feed baskets, which I had been carrying on my shoulders, over my head and placed them on the floor of the barn. I fed the mules a light meal of oats and corn. It was important to keep them healthy and strong so they could pull the canal boat the sixty miles from Easton to tidewater at Bristol.

I pulled the harnesses off the stable wall and placed them around the necks of Daisy and Belle. By then they had finished their breakfast and it was time to put their bridles over their heads and their bits in their mouths.

I always thought that the hardest part of taking care of the mules was placing the bits in their mouths. Daisy and Belle would always try to spit them out, just like George did when Mama tried to give him castor oil when he was sick.

The reins for the mules were connected to the bridle. They were one long, endless strap that went from one side of the bridle over the mane and connected to the other side of the bit. I regularly checked the mules' shoes, even though I knew Daddy always checked them at the beginning of every canal season. I had to get into the habit of checking the shoes after each trip. "You don't like walking around with holes in your shoes, Anna, do you?" Daddy would say.

Sometimes when the winter snow melted in the mountains in early spring, a flood of water would damage the canal, delaying the beginning of the season. Spring freshets would not prevent the canal season from beginning on time in the spring of 1862.

That April morning after I finished getting the mules ready for Daddy and John, I helped Mama prepare breakfast for the family. As the oldest daughter I also had to make sure Elizabeth, James, and George were doing their chores and were not fighting. James and George could be very mischievous when they wanted to be and even when they didn't want to be.

I remember one time, when Mama asked them to pull out the weeds in the garden, they pulled out all the carrots and potato spuds. They often chased the goats when they were supposed to be feeding them and scared the eggs right out of the chickens.

I was very excited that year as we began the canal season because that would be the year when I would help drive the mules. Mama would always get Grandpa Joe, who lived over the hill, to take care of the goats and chickens while we were gone.

Daddy said the whole trip from Easton to Bristol would take about four or five days, unless they ran into some trouble. When I asked him what he meant by trouble he said to me, "You'll know what trouble is when you see it, Anna."

Mama and I said goodbye to Daddy and John as they headed into the morning mist. I helped Mama prepare breakfast for my brothers and sister. Most mornings Mama let Elizabeth, James, and George sleep until seven o'clock. I often thought it was because Mama wanted to have at least a couple of hours of peace and quiet before they woke up. But, Mama would never admit that.

Helping my brothers and sister with their chores made the mornings go fast. After the chores were done that morning I asked Mama if I could go see Minnie and tell her all about our upcoming annual family trip down the Delaware Canal.

Chapter Two
• *Minnie* •

I remember stepping off our back porch and running through the trees, thinking of all the wonderful stories Minnie had told me about the canal. Minnie had lived sixty-five years along the canal and had seen more than anyone I had ever known, except perhaps Grandpa Joe.

Minnie's stories were filled with laughter and mystery and made me wish I had been born fifty years sooner. I traveled through the trees and climbed the small hill that led to the meadow on the other side. Below the hill lay a blanket of wildflowers beyond which sat Minnie's house. I often thought that running through the fragrant flowers was my reward for climbing up the hill. I remember the smell of honeysuckle and lavender as I would draw closer to Minnie's.

I would find Minnie sitting on her front porch rocking in her rocking chair. She would weave her stories to the rhythm of the rocker against the wooden planks of the porch. She was always quick to offer a glass of lemonade, as long as you went and got it yourself.

Beyond the house sat the stable where the mules that pulled Minnie's canal boat had been kept.

Minnie's husband and children were long gone, and so too were the mules, but the memories of their life in the early days of the canal were as strong as Minnie's lemonade.

Minnie could tell right away that the day was different than other days because I was so excited to tell her about our annual trip down the canal. Before I even started to tell her, Minnie settled in to reminisce. "I remember our first trip down the canal," she began.

Minnie's children were all long gone, having left years before. Two of her sons lived along the canal and had carried on the tradition of canalling with their families. Minnie's other two sons had moved; one to Easton and one to Philadelphia.

When asked if she ever visited the city, Minnie would reply, "The city is too big for a country girl like me."

Minnie's daughters looked just like her. I knew this because of all the photographs Minnie had perched on her mantel. Their long brown hair pulled up in a tight bun, looked just like Minnie's hair except that her hair was the color of the moon on a winter's night.

Minnie told me to sit for a spell and she began telling me all about their first canal trip. As I settled in to listen to Minnie, I was grateful to be a country girl also, and not a city girl.

Minnie's stories always began at four in the morning, with Maggie and Martha. They were the names of Minnie's mules. I guess if Maggie and Martha hadn't wanted to get up, then the story would end before it began, and Minnie would have just kept rocking.

Just like our family, as Minnie's husband and sons prepared the mules for the sixty-mile journey, Minnie and her daughters would finish baking the bread and preparing the supplies that would sustain them on their long working days. When Minnie did go on a trip she cooked and even steered the boat so her husband and sons could eat. Somehow I couldn't imagine Mama steering the canal boat. But if Minnie could do it, then I knew that Mama could.

As Minnie finished her story, I remember thinking about the short trip I would take from Minnie's house to my friend Susanna's house. First, I would stop at Yoder's General Store to buy some candy to share with Susanna.

Chapter Three
• *Susanna's War* •

As I waved goodbye to Minnie that April day, I realized that morning had turned into early afternoon. I walked through the meadow that led to town and thought about what it would have been like to go to school in a big city and have a teacher that would smile and ask interesting questions. We didn't go to a schoolhouse like some of the other children in the village. Daddy always said that life is the best teacher, next to him and Mama.

Mama read really well and she taught all of us children how to read and write. I ran across the meadow that morning and through the backyards of the houses that would lead me to Yoder's General Store.

I loved going into town. It was so exciting, all of the people walking around going about their business.

The general store was owned and operated by Mr. and Mrs. Yoder. They didn't have any children, so they treated all the children in Smithtown like their own. Mr. Yoder was really nice and would always give me a piece of candy when Mama would send me to the general store for supplies.

Horses and carriages lined the hitching post outside the store and more people than usual seemed to be milling about that April day. A group of adults, including Mr. and Mrs. Yoder, were quietly talking in the corner of the store. I remember overhearing one of them mention President Lincoln's name. President Abraham Lincoln had been inaugurated as the sixteenth president on March 4 of the previous year, 1861. I always remembered that date because March 4 is my birthday.

The adults were in the corner of the room talking about a war that had been raging in places like Fort Sumter and Bull Run. Some of the adults said that the war didn't affect them and they would continue to go about their business as usual.

Mr. Yoder reminded the group that more and more of their sons, brothers, and fathers were called to serve in the war. At the time, I wasn't sure what Mr. Yoder had meant by the word "serve." I vowed to ask Mama when I returned home that day.

The group of adults had started to break up and go about their business when Mr. Yoder noticed me standing in the front of the store. He handed me a piece of candy and I remember boldly asking for another piece of candy for my friend Susanna. He smiled as he handed me another piece of candy and said, "The simple pleasures...if only life could stay the same, uninterrupted by war."

I didn't know how to respond to Mr. Yoder, so I just said, "Thank you," and decided I had another question to ask Mama when I returned home.

I left the general store that day, placing the nugget of candy for Susanna in my dress pocket, and adjusting my bonnet to shade my eyes from the afternoon sun.

Susanna and I walked through the yard behind her house and skipped stones in the creek beyond her fence. Susanna didn't talk much that day and at times was downright silent, but when she did talk she told me that her older brother Sam had enlisted and gone off to fight in the war. I wondered if the war that Sam had gone off to fight in was the same war that the people were talking about in Mr. Yoder's store. There can't be two different wars going on at the same time, I thought to myself on that sunny April afternoon.

Susanna seemed sad that day and said that her dad had been talking about giving up his canal boat and going to work for the "Iron Horse," since Sam had gone off to war.

I had even more questions to ask Mama when I went home that day. After skipping all the stones within our reach, we realized that it was getting late. I realized that I had better start home to help Mama with the supper preparations. Susanna thanked me for the candy and off I ran.

As I skipped through the honeysuckle and lavender field that began my journey home I thought about all the people I had seen that day and all the questions I needed to ask Mama.

When I returned home I found Mama washing clothes in the big, round wooden tub that sat in the back of the house near the fence. Elizabeth and James were sitting on the pile of firewood next to Mama. George was busy chasing the goats around the pen.

Mama reminded me that it was late afternoon and I should have been home hours ago to help her with the wash. I apologized and explained to her that I had been to Minnie's house and Susanna's house.

I told Mama about the adults talking at Mr. Yoder's general store and I asked her, "What is an 'Iron Horse'? Is it really a horse made of iron?"

She told me that an Iron Horse is a railroad car. "Those cars that ride on the railroad tracks."

"What's inside a railroad car?" I asked.

"All kinds of things can be inside a railroad car."

"Things like the coal that Daddy and John carry in their boat?" I asked.

"Yes, things like the coal Daddy and John carry in their boat," she answered.

I told Mama that Susanna's dad might stop being a steersman and get a job with the railroad because that's where the future was.

"Well," Mama said. "Some people think the way Susanna's dad does, and others like your father think that there is still a need for the Delaware Canal and canal boats."

Susanna was also very sad because her brother Sam had gone off to fight in the war. I remember thinking that her brother was just a couple of years older than John.

"Could John go off and fight in the war?" I asked.

Mama's smile left her face, and she too started to look sad. "I hope not, Anna."

She became very quiet and didn't even notice when George chased a chicken right through some of the wash that she had just finished.

Chapter Four
• *Safe Return* •

Four days had passed. The day that Daddy and John would return from their first canal trip had finally arrived. We all hoped that they would return home before we went to bed so we could hear all about their trip.

Mama spent the day going about her chores, but I could tell she was even more anxious than we were to see Daddy and John. I always thought that first canal trip of the season was the hardest for Mama to bear. It seemed like they had been away for weeks, but it had only been four days.

Mama sent me to the general store to order supplies that we would need for our first trip down the canal as a family. I remember thinking that Mama had sent me on that chore just to get me out of her hair. I kept asking her questions about our trip, which I think was driving her crazy.

When I arrived at Mr. Yoder's store with my list in my hand, he assured me that he would have all the supplies we would need in time for our trip, from the oats for the mules to the candy for me and my brothers and sister. I don't remember Mama ever putting candy on the list.

"That's all I need to know," I said.

Mr. Yoder laughed and handed me a nugget of candy. Mr. Yoder knew me very well, I told Mama when I returned home that day.

"I know you better," she said, "and I know you have been avoiding cleaning the stable, so you better get to it before your father returns home tonight. You know how he feels about a messy stable."

It was my job to keep the stable in order and the mules well cared for. I was responsible for making sure there were enough oats and feed for the mules and keeping the bridles and harnesses clean and in working order.

Mules were the best animals for pulling canal boats because they are strong and surefooted and can walk for many hours, outlasting a horse. Horses liked to stop and eat from the trees on the side of the towpath, mules wouldn't. Horses were faster than mules, but they would get excited easier and like water more than mules. A horse would head straight into the canal water to cool off.

You could smell the stable long before you stepped foot in it. The reins from the bridle fell to the floor in a cascade of smooth, brown leather. An extra feed basket hung in the corner of the stable grateful to be hanging there instead of in front of a mule's face. An old worn collar hung from a peg on the stable wall. A collar was worn around a mule's neck, and strapped to each side were wooden hames to which traces were attached.

Also, on the collar was a leather houser. The houser had two holes in it, for the ends of the hames to pass through, and it covered the top of the collar to keep the rain off the mules' shoulders. Daddy used leather to cover their shoulders instead of canvas because he always said that the mules' shoulders are an important part of their body and must be taken care of.

On the wooden table against the wall sat brushes in various shapes and sizes, a branding iron, and old horseshoes. Missing from the table was my favorite accessory for the mules, their bells.

The bells hung from the bottom of their collar on a string about one and one-half inches wide. The bells would warn the lock tender of an approaching boat.

Fly nets were used to protect the mules from flies. Extra nets were draped over pegs on the wall, suspended like giant spider webs waiting to catch their prey. I had gotten so involved with cleaning the stable that I didn't realize that day had turned to dusk.

Mama held supper a little later than normal in the hope that Daddy and John would return in time to eat with us. As if thinking about something could make it happen, I turned to find Daddy and John standing in front of the stable with Daisy and Belle.

I ran up to greet them and quickly noticed the exhaustion on their dirt-covered faces. Daddy gave me a hug and John greeted me with a '"Hi, kid," as they handed the mules over to my care and headed off toward the house. Even Daisy and Belle looked tired that April evening.

George and Elizabeth heard the mules' bells and bolted out the back door, anxious to welcome home Daddy and John.

The minute I took the harnesses off Daisy and Belle they lay down in the hay and began the ritual of rolling around on the ground. They twisted their necks and flexed their legs as if they were dancing to a strange song known only to them. I brushed them off when the show ended and prepared their supper as quickly as I could, so that I could go inside and

Canal mules wearing their fly netting and harness

Pennsylvania Canal Society Collection, National Canal Museum, Easton, Pennsylvania. Collection of James Lee

enjoy my supper and hear all about the adventures that would await me on the Delaware Canal.

Mama had prepared a wonderful feast of boiled potatoes and meat, canned vegetables from last year's harvest, and her special white crumb cake, Daddy's favorite.

When supper was over, the family settled in around Daddy as he sat in his rocking chair. He lit his corncob pipe and started to spin the tale of their latest adventure on the canal.

That time, like all other times, he had a captive audience. We just loved the sound of his voice as he told us about all the people he met and the places he had seen on his canal journey—a journey that our family would soon take together.

Chapter Five
• *Bloody Battles* •

The next few weeks were a hectic time for our family. Mama busied herself with the preparations for our trip, canning and getting our supplies in order. I never realized how many supplies Daddy and John took with them on their trips. Of course, for this journey we took supplies for seven people, not two.

Our trip would begin in three days and Mama was counting supplies we had on hand, making note of what was still needed from Yoder's General Store. Supplies included bacon, ham, butter, coffee, brown sugar, potatoes, and, of course, oats for the team. We also had to carry hay on the trip so we could stable the mules overnight. I liked going into town for supplies because I knew Mr. Yoder would reward me with a nugget of candy.

With my list in hand, I set out that morning on my chore of gathering supplies from town. I asked

Mama if I could stop at Susanna's first and enlist her help in carrying the supplies home.

Mama said, "Fine, as long as you don't dawdle."

When I arrived at Susanna's house she seemed happier than she was my last visit. She had just received word that her brother Sam was fine and not to worry.

Susanna and I jumped from stone to stone across the stream that morning as the water threatened to soak our shoes. We skipped across the meadow and headed toward town. We were close to town when Susanna asked me, "What do you want to do when you get older, Anna?"

I said, "I really haven't thought about it much, but I know I love listening to Mama read to me from one of her books." My favorite book was *Flower Fables* by Louisa May Alcott. It had been given to Mama by her mother a couple of weeks before she died.

"I think I would like to write stories that people could read over and over again," I said.

Susanna said that she liked watching Doc Johnson take care of people and wanted to work with a doctor someday.

From a distance we could see a boat gliding down the canal guided by a team of mules. We waved to the steersman, and I noticed that the letters on the back of the boat were the same as the letters on the back of the boat that Daddy steered, L.C. & Nav. Co. I knew that this stood for Lehigh Coal & Navigation Company; the only difference was that the numbers on Daddy's boat were 526 and the numbers on this boat read 116.

We continued on our journey that warm May morning and arrived at Mr. Yoder's general store, stopping first to admire the horses that lined the hitching post like soldiers standing at attention. We set about our task of finding the items on the list. We had found most of the items when I noticed Susanna standing perfectly still, listening to a couple of women who were talking in the corner of the store. As I drew closer I could hear what they were saying.

They were talking about the Civil War and two great ships made of iron, the *Merrimac* and the *Monitor.* I remember thinking, Why is everything made of iron? They continued, "a bloody battle at Williamsburg and Fair Oaks has maimed many soldiers and killed even more."

I looked over at Susanna just as they had said the word "killed" and watched as her face turned from the color of the morning sun to the gray of a stormy day. The two potatoes she was holding in her hands fell to the floor with a loud thud.

It was then that the women turned around and gasped, holding their hands over their mouths. But the damage had been done. Susanna bolted out the door of the general store and ran across the dirt road. She crossed the meadow faster than ever before, as I called after her to stop. When we had finally run out of wind, we collapsed in the field. As I came closer to her I could see the tears streaming down her face.

"Anna, I'm scared," she sobbed.

We sat for what seemed like hours, and when we finally did get up to walk home silence surrounded us like a blanket of thick fog.

By the time I returned home later that afternoon, it was supper time and my family had just started to say grace.

"Anna, where have you been, and why don't you have the supplies your mother sent you for?" Daddy asked.

I told them what had happened at Mr. Yoder's store and how upset Susanna had become when the women were talking about the war.

John said, "I can't wait to be drafted so I can go serve in the war."

Mama said, "Bite your tongue. May this war end long before you reach the age of draft."

Daddy said, "I think this war will touch all of us sooner or later in one way or another." Again, a silence came over the room. Why is it that when people talked about the war everyone got so quiet?

I promised Mama that I would go back to the store the next day to get the supplies we needed, but first I would stop at Susanna's house and make sure she was all right.

Chapter Six

• *Our Trip Begins* •

The day had finally arrived when we would begin our trip down the canal. I was awake before dawn, eager for our journey to begin. Elizabeth, James, and even George required little prodding that morning to get out of bed. As we all scurried about, busy with last-minute preparations, John loaded the supplies onto the L.C. & Nav. Co. No. 526 boat.

This was what I had been waiting for all year. This would be the year when I would drive the team more than ever before. Daddy told me that John would soon be heading out on his own and driving the team would be my job. Mama wanted to believe that John heading out meant he was going to Easton to work at a newspaper, but Daddy never said that. I often wondered if Daddy thought the Civil War would last until John was old enough to serve.

Our journey began in Easton at the confluence of the Delaware and Lehigh Rivers. As I stood on the deck of the section boat and gazed at the buildings of Easton I could see why John had become so captivated by this city. The tall buildings had many windows, and each window seemed to tell a different story. Church steeples reached toward the sky like giant flowers stretching toward the sun.

Our boat was a section boat, which meant that it was divided into two sections that could be separated in the middle for loading, unloading, and turning the boat. The boat had been loaded with coal at Mauch Chunk. Daddy relieved the driver from the first leg of the journey at Easton. The trip from Easton to tidewater at Bristol would take about four days.

The return trip was always faster because the boat traveled only about two miles an hour when it was loaded with coal. A light boat or unloaded boat could be pulled much faster and travel the distance faster.

On the deck, at the stern, standing at attention was the "night-hawker." The night-hawker was an oil lamp with a polished reflector that sat in what looked like a box. The box was twelve to fourteen inches high, surrounded by glass on three sides, and hung from the "dasher." The night-hawker would give us light and help guide us down the canal at night.

Sectional hatches protected the coal and prevented water from getting into the bilge. There was an area surrounding the hatches where you could walk around, but John warned to be careful because sometimes it could be tricky in rough water.

Along the sides of the boat on both sections were two cleats. The cleats were used for attaching the towline, and snubbing when we passed through a lock.

Sometimes when it rained really hard, water would get into the bilge. Each section of the boat had one pump for removing water from the bilge.

On the deck near the hinges was a barrel for drinking water and a feed basket that held the oats and feed for the mules.

L.C. & Nav. Co. 526 had two stoves, one on the deck and the other in the cabin.

Lying along the top of the deck was the hook pole. It looked just like it sounds. On one end of the pole was a steel rod with a hook.

The hook pole was used for moving the boat along a wharf, for pushing or changing the location of the boat when the mules weren't available, and for vaulting to and from the towpath.

There was a compartment under the fore deck to store rope and other gear. The stern of the boat was where the tiller was located. The tiller is what steered the boat and where Daddy spent most of his time. The tiller was connected to the rudderpost, which stuck out from the back of the boat like a giant fin.

Under the stern deck was the cabin that would become our home away from home for the length of the trip. Mama hung curtains on the two small windows in the cabin. This was her way of trying to make the boat seem more like home. The cabin was only eight feet by ten feet, and I wondered how our family of seven would ever live in this small area.

There were two bunks, an upper and a lower. The bunks were on hinges so that they could be raised against the wall when not in use.

Daddy announced that the men would sleep on the deck and the women in the cabin. Mama would sleep in one bunk and Elizabeth and I would share the other one.

At the stern of the boat was a locker for storing food. The bottom of the locker was below the water line of the boat so the food wouldn't spoil. A hinged table dropped over the locker, and when we were not using it, it too went up against the wall.

On one wall was a cupboard for dishes and kitchen utensils. In the front of the cabin, opposite the bunks, was the place where Mama spent most of her time—at the stove.

Daddy called the stove "a boatsman choice." The stove had two griddles on top and the words "Orr, Painter and Company, Reading, Pennsylvania" written on the side.

A door in front of the cabin led to the cargo hold. Mama would hang wash in the cargo hold during the return trip when the bilge was empty if the weather turned stormy.

The cabin was below the deck and was illuminated by oil lamps mounted on the wall.

Our trip began with the sound of little feet exploring the boat, the smell of Mama's cooking in the cabin, and the sight of Daddy standing at the tiller while John led the team on the towpath.

Section boat tied up at New Hope

Lock tender's house in right background is now a visitor's center
and headquarters of Friends of the Delaware Canal.

Deck of a section boat

The photograph shows the feed box and equipment locker, water barrel, coal bin, and boatman's cook plate iron stove.

Pennsylvania Canal Society Collection, National Canal Museum, Easton, Pennsylvania

Chapter Seven
• *Driving the Team* •

The first lock we passed through was a weigh lock or Lock No. 24. The lock tender helped Daddy guide the boat into the lock area, and I watched in amazement as the water level around the boat became lower and lower.

The water disappeared and the boat was sitting on a huge scale. The scale was under the boat, and it weighed the boat with all the coal in it. The lock tender handed John a slip of paper with numbers written on it. The numbers told the steersman how much the boat weighed, the date, and the time of day that the boat passed through the lock.

The slip of paper had the number 90 written on the bottom. When I asked John what that meant, he said, "Our boat now weighs 90 tons." At the time I couldn't even imagine how heavy that was.

As John led the team down the twelve-foot-wide towpath, the bells on Daisy and Belle rang with constant rhythm.

When we left the lock, Daddy began navigating the canal while Mama continued to cook breakfast in the cabin. The smell of bacon wafted through the air and awakened my senses. It was then that I realized that I had been daydreaming when I should have been helping Mama.

"Anna, where have you been? I need your help," Mama said. "Please go get me fresh water for coffee."

Breakfast always tasted better when we were traveling on the canal. Mama prepared a tasty breakfast of bacon and eggs with homemade bread and butter. By the time we had finished cleaning up from breakfast that morning, we were coming up on the next two locks. George and James continued to run around the deck while Elizabeth tried very hard to read the signs that hung above the locks.

"Lock No. 23 and Lock No. 22 at Raubsville," she announced to everyone as we drew closer. I finally had a chance to sit down and found a seat atop the toolbox at the stern of the boat.

It was the middle of May and the trees were covered with a thick coat of leaves. I remember hearing the birds chirp and watching the squirrels and rabbits dart from tree to tree trying to find food.

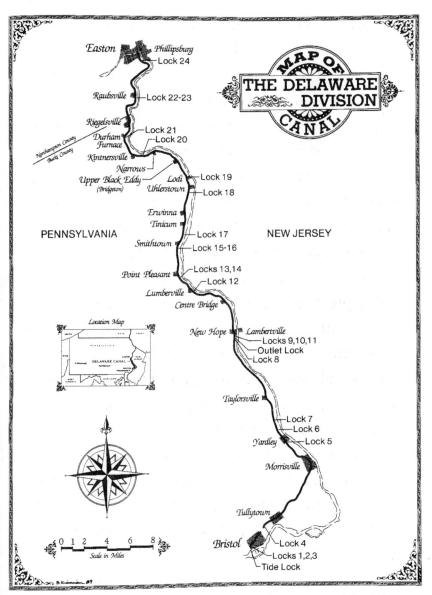

Easton — Phillipsburg
└ Lock 24

Raubsville ▮ └ Lock 22-23

Riegelsville ▮
Durham └ Lock 21
Furnace └ Lock 20

Northampton County
Bucks County

Kintnersville

Narrows
Upper Black Eddy — Lodi — Lock 19
(Bridgeton) — Uhlerstown — Lock 18

Erwinna
Tinicum
Lock 17
Smithtown └ Lock 15-16

PENNSYLVANIA   **NEW JERSEY**

Locks 13,14
Point Pleasant ▮ └ Lock 12
Lumberville ▮
Centre Bridge ▮

New Hope ▮ — Lambertville
└ Locks 9,10,11
└ Outlet Lock
└ Lock 8

Taylorsville

└ Lock 7
└ Lock 6
Yardley ▮ └ Lock 5
Morrisville

Tullytown

Bristol — Lock 4
└ Locks 1,2,3
└ Tide Lock

MAP OF THE DELAWARE DIVISION CANAL

Location Map

DELAWARE CANAL

0 1 2   4   6   8
Scale in Miles

B. Küvvvien 89

Pennsylvania Canal Society Collection, National Canal Museum,
Easton, Pennsylvania

I couldn't see it, but I knew that on the other side of the trees ran the Delaware River. Lumber was once taken down the Delaware River to Bristol on rafts. The river was too difficult to navigate and even harder to navigate when the rafts had to come up the river, so the canal was built.

The next town we came to was Riegelsville. Mama joined us up on the deck just as Daddy said, "There was a coal yard and a dock in Riegelsville, but all the wheeling and dealing is done at W. Walters' saloon."

When I asked him what a saloon was, he said, "It's a place to mix business with beer and grog."

About a mile or so down the canal sat the community of Durham Furnace Works. I could see yellow and blue shops lining the street and ladies in fancy dresses with big hats parading up and down the berm side of the canal.

When we came closer to Lock No. 21, I noticed that the boat seemed to be moving above the water, as if we were flying in the air. It was at Lock No. 21 that the Delaware Canal crossed over the Durham Creek.

"The reason you feel like you're flying, Anna," Daddy said, as he eased the boat into the lock, "is because we are traveling over an aqueduct."

"What is an aqueduct?" I asked.

"An aqueduct is a road made of steel, stone, or wood that will help our boat travel over the creek."

"The Delaware Canal is full of wonders," I told Daddy.

"Yes, Anna, it is!"

The next town we came to was Kintersville. Many of the canal workers lived in and around this town. I remember Mama telling me that she had lived in Kintersville with Daddy and John before I was born.

Daddy asked me to get the feedbags ready for the team. The mules ate four times a day.

Daddy blew into the conch shell, signalling to the lock tender that our boat was approaching the lock.

I heard a loud voice telling Daddy to hold up because the gates were open. The lock tender moved to the lock shanty and opened the middle wickets to fill the lock with water. When it was safe to move into the lock, Daddy threw out a line with a loop on it to John. John placed the line over a cleat along the side of the lock. Daddy "snubbed" the rope around the boat cleat to stop the boat before it hit the lower gates. The boat sank into the lock as Daddy loosened the rope. Before I knew it, the lower gates opened and we were leaving the lock.

Upper mitre gates. Lock at New Hope.

Pennsylvania Canal Society Collection, National Canal Museum, Easton, Pennsylvania

After we left the lock I asked Daddy, "How does a lock work?"

He explained, "There are five types of locks: the weigh lock at Easton, guard locks that help control water levels in the canal during spring freshets to avoid flooding, outlet locks that provide access from a canal into a river, tide locks that help us into the river at tidewater, and last but not least lift locks that work by raising or lowering a boat from one level to another."

Daddy had just finished explaining the difference between the locks when James and George came running down the side of the deck. Daddy yelled, "Stop, before one of you ends up in the canal and we have to fish you out like a shad in the river."

A cornucopia of smells rose up from the cabin that afternoon as Mama prepared dinner. She had placed salt pork in the stew pot and asked me to add potatoes and carrots to the stew while she cut up a head of cabbage.

Up on deck James and George had stopped running long enough to help Elizabeth husk the corn.

We finished dinner, and Daddy asked me to go relieve John on the towpath so he could eat dinner.

"How will I get there, swim?" I asked.

"No, silly, you vault. You take this pole and vault to the towpath, and John will vault back onto the boat."

I had never vaulted before, so Daddy steered the boat as close as he could to the towpath without getting the boat stuck in the silt.

After John finished eating he called to me on the towpath and asked if I was ready to come back to the boat. I called to him that I would like to drive the team longer. I liked walking with the mules, and the feeling of solid ground under my feet.

We passed the town of Narrows and began to near Upper Black Eddy. Upper Black Eddy was also known as Bridgeton. There was a general store and a boatyard in Upper Black Eddy.

I remember seeing something that resembled a huge skeleton of a boat in the distance surrounded by men who looked like they were putting together a huge puzzle. This was the boatyard Daddy talked about.

Mama, who had come up from the cabin said, "I heard there are two hotels in Bridgeton." I had never seen a hotel before.

Daddy asked me to stay on the towpath and watch what happened when we got to the next lock.

Chapter Eight
• *The Iron Horse* •

As we drew closer to Lock 19 at Lodi, John spotted the snubbing post. He asked Daddy to throw him the line from the boat. I asked what he was doing and he told me that he would attach the line from the boat to the snubbing post so he could get the boat to slow down, as it got closer to the lock.

He said, "You don't want to go into the lock too fast, Anna."

John snubbed the boat, slacked off as the water level went down, and then unhooked the line. He ran down along the lock and pulled the line so it wouldn't get snagged. He pulled on two wickets on the lower gates to help the lock tender pull the drop gate. As the gate went up, he pulled all the other wickets on the lower gates.

The mules continued walking down the towpath. John had asked me to stop the team downstream.

Passing through Lock 19 at Lodi. Dasher with night-hawker.

Pennsylvania Canal Society Collection, National Canal Museum, Easton, Pennsylvania

The mules walked past the lock and stopped without any effort from me. It only took about three or four minutes for Daddy to bring the boat through the lock.

When John finished helping the lock tender he met me and the team farther down the towpath. Daddy threw John the line and he reattached it to the mules.

The next lock was just a couple of miles away, so I decided to keep walking on the towpath with John and the team.

John asked if I minded if he jumped back on the boat to get a drink of water. It was mid-afternoon and the sun was high and hot.

The next town we came to was Ulherstown. I remember Daddy telling me that there were limekilns in Ulherstown. I didn't know what a limekiln was, so I asked John when he came back from getting his drink.

He told me that limekilns were places where limestone is burned or calcinated. Once the limestone was burned, it was used for farm fertilizer or cement. Sometimes limewater was used to whitewash barns, chicken houses, or fences. He even told me the story of a man who would take a chunk of lime and put it into his jar of water. The limestone would dissolve and then he would drink the water. I often wonder if

**The canal boat of "Erv" Grant Emery near Uhlertown.
He always used two mules and one white horse.**

that story was true or whether John was just pulling my leg.

My legs grew tired, so John hoisted me up onto Daisy's back. While he lifted me in the air he said. "Your chariot awaits, dear Anna."

I felt like a princess riding on top of Daisy. I'm not sure how Daisy felt about carrying royalty. The view from atop the mule was different from the view on the towpath. I was enjoying the sounds of the canal and the repetition of the clippity clop of the mules' shoes on the towpath, when all of a sudden I heard a loud splash in the canal behind us.

George had fallen off the boat and into the canal just as Daddy had predicted. Mama came running up from the cabin just as John jumped into the canal and pulled George out from under the water. John swung George back onto the boat. From the towpath I could hear Daddy yelling, "I told you two to stop running around the deck. Now go downstairs and dry off in front of the stove."

I was glad to be riding on my chariot on the towpath and not on the boat with Daddy. A few miles down the towpath my bottom was starting to hurt from sitting on Daisy. I thought about going back on the boat and hoped that Daddy was over being mad, even though he wasn't mad at me.

As we traveled from Ulherstown to Erwinna I could once again smell Mama's cooking. Supper was leftovers from dinner and Mama's famous coffeebruckle.

I used the pole to vault back onto the boat, hoping I wouldn't miss and land in the water.

While Mama and I prepared supper in the cabin, I remember hearing Daddy talking to the steersman of a passing boat.

It seemed that every time another boat passed, I was down in the cabin. "Don't worry, Anna, we still have three days left on our trip. You'll see a boat pass us sooner or later," Mama reassured me.

Daddy sent John into the cabin to eat first since he had eaten dinner last. After John finished he went back up on the deck to handle the tiller.

By the time Mama and I had cleaned up from dinner and emerged from the cabin the day had turned to dusk.

Daddy told us that in a few hours we would stop for the day at Tinicum. "There's a nice stable there for the mules," he said. It was about ten o'clock at night when we snubbed right outside of Moore Stables, just shy of Tinicum.

I helped John walk the mules to the stable while Mama helped James, George, and Elizabeth get ready for bed. As we walked down the towpath we could hear the sweet sounds of Mama's violin accompanying a chorus of crickets.

James and George were fast asleep on the deck when we returned from the stable. Daddy carried the boys downstairs. He said it would be best if they slept down in the cabin with us because of the night air.

I had to admit that night that I was really tired and I followed Elizabeth to bed. As I lay in the bunk listening to the night sounds of the canal I could hear Daddy and John arguing with each other about the "Iron Horse."

I remember as if it were yesterday, John yelling at Daddy, "Didn't you notice all the train tracks we passed? The railroad is the future, not the canal."

Daddy's voice was even louder. "Boy, you don't know what you're talking about. Your grandfather built this canal, and it's provided a good living for his family and for our family. This canal ain't going anywhere."

I heard John's footsteps march across the deck and fade into the night.

Chapter Nine
• *Passing Friends* •

The sound of a passing boat woke me up the next morning. By the time I had made my way up on deck, the boat had passed, again.

Daddy was at the tiller and John was already on the towpath with the mules. I hoped that Daddy wasn't still mad at John.

The sights, sounds, and smells of the Delaware Canal greeted us on the second day of our trip.

When everyone was awake, we ate breakfast and looked forward to passing our hometown of Smithtown.

When we passed through Lock No. 17 and heading past Smithtown we were greeted by a group of our neighbors and friends standing on the berm side of the bank. Susanna was standing along the side of the canal waving her arms and shouting, "Good luck. See you in a couple of days."

Soon after we passed Smithtown we came to Locks No. 15 and 16.

Daddy reached into the toolbox on the deck and pulled out the conch shell. He asked me if wanted to signal to the lock tender and handed me the shell. It was huge in my small hand and I had to hold it with two hands so it didn't fall into the canal.

Daddy instructed me, "You have to blow really hard, Anna."

I blew into the shell as hard as I could. It sounded like a cat purring. Daddy laughed and said, "Blow hard."

I took a deep breath and blew with all my might. That time instead of a cat purring, I heard a cow mooing.

Daddy said, "Well, that's better, but do you think they know we're coming?"

"I don't think so," I said.

He gently took the shell from my hands, placed it to his lips, took a deep breath and blew. I heard the long, loud sound of a foghorn.

As we made our way through Lock No. 16 and Lock No. 15, I watched every move John made, so that the next year, when it was my job to drive the mules, I would know just what to do.

The sun kept peaking in and out of the clouds and it looked like it was going to start raining.

The next town on the trip was Point Pleasant. Daddy reminded us that the Point Pleasant area was a maze of waterways, bridges, and roads. "There's a lot of hustle and bustle," he said, "so we have to be mindful of what we're doing."

Even Mama, who spent most of her time in the cabin, came up on deck to see what all the excitement was about. The closer we came to the lock the more activity I could see. There was a family of five picnicking along the bank of the canal.

The next lock on the canal was at Lumberville. Because this part of the canal was so close to the river, floods caused a great deal of damage to this area. There was a large sawmill and lumberyard near town; I guess that's why they called it Lumberville.

In the distance I could see the lock tender standing next to the "doghouse." I never understood why it was called a doghouse when there was no dog in it. Perhaps, it was called a "doghouse" because that was what it looked like. Daddy explained to me that the lock tender turns a handle that sticks out of the doghouse.

The handle turned a cog that fitted into a rack bar attached to the "doghouse." Heavy wheels on the top of the gates controlled the gate wickets that allowed the water to flow in and out of the lock.

A long, red, covered bridge led across the river to an island. Mama told me that the island is called Bulls Island and it was really on the New Jersey side of the river.

"You have to pay to go over the bridge. It's the most traveled bridge crossing the Delaware River," she explained. "There's a feeder canal that leads to the Raritan Canal on the other side of Bulls Island."

We had just enough time to eat dinner before we came to the next town, Center Bridge. I saw another covered bridge in the distance; that one led to Stockton, New Jersey.

John once told me that sometimes they would stop at a place called the "Cake and Beer House" when they got to Center Bridge. I wondered if Daddy ever told Mama that they stopped at the "Cake and Beer House."

About an hour after we left Center Bridge, I saw another boat coming toward us from the opposite direction. I'd finally get to see what I'd been waiting for: another boat passing from the opposite direction. Mama said if I waited long enough it was bound to happen. As usual Mama was right. I could tell that the boat passing us was lighter and didn't have any cargo in its hull because it was sitting higher in the water than our boat. That meant that the other boat had the right of way.

Daddy steered our boat to the berm side of the canal. Our mules stopped, and the towline sank to the bottom of the canal.

The mules from the other boat passed over the towline. When the boat had passed, our team started heading back down the path, and once again we were on our way.

With the excitement of Center Bridge and the passing boat behind us we all settled on the deck to relax for a time. The clouds had disappeared and the hot sun gave Mama cause to retrieve her bonnet from the cabin.

Daddy announced to everyone that we should enjoy the view because soon we'd be at New Hope where there are four locks.

Even the boys stopped running and basked in the afternoon sun. Their rest was short-lived, and before long they were running up and down the deck playing tag.

Elizabeth and I counted the different kinds of birds we saw flying from branch to branch. There were cardinals, blue jays, and other brightly colored

**Molly Polly Chunker Expedition.
Children on the canal boat at Weissport.**

Pennsylvania Canal Society Collection, National Canal Museum,
Easton, Pennsylvania. Photograph by Louis Tiffany, 1880s

birds trying to find the best branch to rest on. Squirrels and rabbits also scurried from bush to bush searching for nuts and berries. Once in a while we would see a house off in the distance with children playing in the yard and wash hanging on the line. My mind wandered to Minnie, and how I couldn't wait to see her to tell her all about our trip.

Before I knew it, we were coming up on New Hope and Daddy shouted, "All hands on deck. We may need everyone's help to get through New Hope." There were four locks in New Hope, but Mama only wanted to know about the shops in town. She watched as women passed by in their brightly colored dresses and fancy hats.

All the locks in New Hope were double locks, even though most of the locks on the Delaware Canal were single locks.

I asked why the locks in New Hope were different, and Daddy replied, "The locks in New Hope are double locks so that two boats can pass through the lock at the same time side by side."

There were so many boats waiting to pass through the locks that it looked to me like they should have a lock that four boats could pass through at once. We signaled to the lock tender that we were ready to enter the lock. We made our way through Lock No. 11 toward Lock No. 10. A barge was tied to the side waiting to be loaded with lumber to be sent to Bristol.

New Hope was a big town, and they even had a trolley car that ran next to the canal down River Road.

When we came closer to Lock No. 10, the lock tender told Daddy that we had to wait for the next boat to get into the lock with us so we could pass through together.

Daddy told us to keep a sharp eye out for what happens at the "Toll House," at Lock No. 9. The collector, Mr. Warford, measured the draft of our boat so he could figure out how much our boat weighed.

He asked Daddy where we were going, "Will it be the Bristol Basin or the Raritan Canal?" Mr. Warford then walked into the "Toll House" and recorded the charges for our boat in his book.

If we were going to the Raritan Canal, Mr. Warford would have raised a red flag to signal to the people on the New Jersey side of the river that a boat was coming across the river.

Mama wasn't interested in anything Mr. Warford was doing and just wanted to know when she could come back to New Hope to shop.

"Someday soon, Margaret, I promise," Daddy answered.

The last lock we passed through in the New Hope area was Lock No. 8. I remember a red building with a sign hanging above the door that read "The River House."

Daddy was right; between all the excitement of New Hope and the afternoon sun we were all tired by early evening. After we cleaned up from supper, Mama opened the bench and pulled out a book.

Mama loved reading to us, and on such a beautiful night she suggested that we all go up on deck with blankets and enjoy the night sky while she read to us. She read by the light of the "night-hawker," as it lit the towpath ahead. Daddy was at the tiller; John was off in the distance sitting on Daisy, as we listened to Mama as she read *Moby Dick* by Herman Melville.

Chapter Ten
• *Fifteen Cents a Tail* •

The morning sun was shining and a gentle breeze was swaying the trees when I came up from the cabin the third day of our trip. Daddy, as always, was at the tiller, and John was dutifully driving the team on the towpath. That would be the day when I would drive the team more than ever before.

I finished breakfast, and vaulted to the towpath so John could eat also.

Daisy and Belle were eating their breakfast from the feed baskets as they plodded along the towpath. The view from the towpath was so different from the view from the boat.

I noticed small animals like chipmunks and finally caught a glance of the muskrats that burrow along the side of the canal. I remember John telling me to keep my eye out for muskrats; they built nests under the towpath. This was dangerous for the mules; a leg could go through the hole and break.

Daddy said, "If you see a muskrat nest, Anna, try and remember where it is so the bank boss can plug it up with straw and mud." The muskrat holes had to be plugged up each season so that the water didn't leak out of the canal. The Lehigh Coal and Navigation Company paid fifteen cents for the end of a muskrat's tail.

I walked along the towpath talking to the mules and keeping an eye on their feed baskets that May morning. Once in awhile when they stopped eating, their bit would fall back into their mouths.

In the distance I heard the sounds of the "Iron Horse." The high pitch sound of the whistle kept blowing and blowing. Every time I heard the whistle I looked over at Daddy and John. They both looked like they wanted to say something, but knew it was best if they didn't.

Late morning turned into early afternoon, and the sun had changed from a light yellow to a bright orange as we passed the town of Taylorsville. Our boat glided across another aqueduct as we crossed over the Jericho Creek.

A group of children were playing on the berm side of the canal. Girls twirled around in flowered dresses edged with ruffles and wide-brimmed hats that kept the afternoon sun off their faces. This of course caught the attention of James and George, who had been running around the deck. They waved their arms and jumped up and down in excitement.

Watching the children play made me think of Susanna and how she often looked sad and worried. I was sure that it was her brother Sam who was on her mind and wondered if her family had heard from him lately.

We passed through Lock No. 7 and Lock No. 6 as I handled the team without any help from John.

Daddy called over to me, "Hey, driver, your relief is on his way." I remember thinking, Daddy just called me a driver.

John vaulted from the boat onto the towpath and told me to go get some food. "You earned it," he said.

Mama and I had just finished the dinner dishes when Daddy called below to tell us that we were coming up on Yardley. A row of buildings lined the street just beyond the berm bank.

Daddy said to Mama, "If you'd like we can tie up just past Lock No. 5 and you and the children can go to some of the shops in Yardley."

Before Mama had a chance to answer, we all cried, "Mama, please say yes, please."

"Very well," she agreed, "it will be good to get my land legs back."

"We won't stop for too long," Daddy bellowed, "just long enough to pick up some supplies."

Mama told all of us to go downstairs and get cleaned up.

Daddy and John guided us through Lock No. 5, and we snubbed up to a post. John stayed with the boat and the mules. Quickly a group of young ladies had gathered around John, who enjoyed all the attention.

Daddy pointed us in the direction of the general store, and we started running before he even finished his sentence.

"Slow down," Mama called after us, "someone will get hurt."

The general store looked so much like Mr. Yoder's general store that I expected to see him standing there with a nugget of candy in his hand. The general store had most of the same things that he had in his store except for one thing. In the corner of the store, on top of a white table sat bolts of beautiful, shiny material carefully folded one on top of the other. Mama spotted the hue of colors as soon as she walked through the door and headed straight for the table. She picked up a bright blue bolt of material and held it up to her cheek, rubbing it slowly from side to side.

"Feel this, Anna. It feels wonderful."

"And looks pretty too," I said.

There was a stack of newspapers on the counter. *The Doylestown Intelligencer* was written across the top of the newspapers.

I overheard the store clerk talking to Daddy. He asked him, "Did you hear of the battle at Norfolk and the burning of the *Merrimac* to prevent its capture?"

It was obvious that Daddy didn't want to be involved in the conversation about the Civil War, but the clerk continued, "The Federals occupy Baton Rouge but were driven out of Fort Royal, Virginia. Thousands have died already and thousands more will before this war is over."

I didn't think anything could have stopped Mama from admiring the beautiful bolts of cloth, but I was wrong. When she heard the clerk say that thousands had been killed and even more would die, she slowly laid the cloth on the table, gathered all of us together, and announced, "It's time to go back to the boat."

Daddy finished paying for the supplies and met us on the boat. John asked me why Mama looked so sad. I didn't know what to tell him, because I didn't understand the whole war thing myself.

The next few miles on the canal were very quiet. Daddy had bought some candy at the general store and passed it out to all of us. He even tossed a couple of pieces to John on the towpath. The four of us sat on the deck, eating our candy while Mama spent the afternoon down in the cabin keeping busy.

We passed through Morrisville on our way to Bristol. Daddy said, "We're coming closer to the end of the canal, Anna."

"What will we do with our coal when we get to Bristol?" I asked.

"The boat will be towed to Philadelphia with us on it and the coal will be unloaded. Then we will be towed back to Bristol. First, we'll tie up in Tullytown for the night, stable the mules, and get an early start tomorrow, so we can get through the last four locks at Bristol early in the morning."

As the warmth of the day turned into the cool of night, through the light of the night-hawker I could see John walking as close to Daisy as he could to keep warm. I lay back on the deck, looked up at the moon, and wondered if Susanna's brother Sam was looking up at the moon, wherever he was.

Chapter Eleven
• *Tidewater at Bristol* •

Before we reached the last three locks, Daddy told me that we had to pass two bridges called "swing" bridges, but most boatman called them "bump" bridges. Between the swing bridges sat a big building called the Grundy Mill.

I asked why the bridges were called bump bridges and Daddy said, "Just watch, Anna, and you'll see why they're called swing bridges or bump bridges."

It looked like he was steering the boat right into the bridge, but the boat bumped into the plank on the side of the bridge and the bridge swung open. After our boat had cleared the bridge, it swung back into place.

Daddy looked at me and said, "Now, do you see why it's called a bump bridge or swing bridge?"

We passed through Lock No. 3 and Lock No. 2. As we headed toward Lock No. 1, I noticed that the canal was making a sharp turn to the left. I could see a large snubbing post ahead where John had stopped the team. He started taking up the slack in the rope, snubbed the boat on the post, and turned the boat around the bend.

Daddy said, "The curve of the canal is too sharp for him to steer the boat around, so we need the snubbing post to turn us so we keep heading into Lock No 1."

We had just finished passing through Lock No. 1 and snubbing the boat when a man named Harry helped John untie the mules and walked off with Daisy and Belle behind him.

"We won't need the team until the return trip, so Harry will take care of them till we get back from Philadelphia. Harry takes good care of the mules," he said. "He cleans them up and even cleans the harnesses and brass."

We had reached tidewater at Bristol.

Daddy announced to everyone, "We'll tie up here for the night and wait for our upriver tow."

The captain of the tug arrived and asked Daddy where we were headed.

He answered, "The Glass House."

I remember thinking, A glass house! I can't wait to see this.

Mama could tell by the look on my face that I thought we were taking the coal to a house made of glass. She said, "Anna, it's not a glass house that people live in. It's a place of business."

The ride up the river gave John a chance to relax since the team was back in Bristol with Harry.

By the time we unloaded our coal and returned to the Bristol Basin it was very late, so Daddy decided we would tie up for the night and begin our journey home very early the next morning. The trip home would be much quicker than the trip down the canal. Our boat would go twice as fast without the coal, four or five miles an hour faster, depending on the mules.

I wanted to sleep late that morning but was woken up early by the sounds coming from other boats tied up in the basin. John had already returned from Harry's with the mules when I stepped up on deck. Daddy was right, they did look well rested and really clean. Even their harnesses looked like they were brand-new.

John and the team pulled us through the first three locks of our return trip home.

James and George wanted to ride on the mules, so John pulled the towline close to the shore, and we all jumped onto the towpath. He gave the boat a push with his foot and it glided toward the center of the canal. As we walked the towpath, I picked beautiful wildflowers from the side of the towpath to give to Mama. Sometimes I could see the river through the trees and hear the rush of the water.

As morning turned into afternoon I could hear the sounds of the "Iron Horse" in the distance. The boys started to complain about riding on top of the hot mules, so John helped them down and they vaulted back onto the boat. They ran down the stairs into the cabin to see what Mama and Elizabeth were doing. The silence of the towpath was a welcome change from the sound of James and George's fighting.

I asked John, "Why do you want to go to Easton?"

"Times are changing, Anna, and the canal isn't going to be around much longer. The railroad can move things faster than we ever could with our boat. Daddy doesn't want to believe it, but the future is in the railroad. Plus, I don't want to spend the rest of my life in Smithtown. Nothing exciting ever happens in Smithtown. I want to write about interesting people and places. Mama and Daddy know that this will be my last season on the canal, even though they won't say it out loud. I think that's why Daddy's asking you to help me so much this trip. This time next year you'll be driving the team, Anna."

I never understood why John wanted to leave Smithtown, but then again I wasn't sixteen.

My feet started to get really tired, so I jumped on top of Belle for a ride. As dinnertime approached we passed Locks No. 9, No. 10, and No. 11.

Daddy thought we would be home by late afternoon if we kept up this pace.

I asked Mama whether I could go see Minnie if we didn't get home too late.

"We'll see," she replied.

As much as I wished our trip on the canal wouldn't end, I was anxious to see Minnie and Susanna.

When we arrived home it was very dark and late. We unloaded the remainder of our supplies. It was too late to go see Minnie or Susanna, so we went to bed. I would go first thing in the morning after I had finished my chores.

Chapter Twelve
• Story to Tell •

I slept later than I wanted to the next morning, and when I asked Mama why she hadn't woken me up earlier, she said I looked so exhausted last night that she thought it would be good for me to sleep in.

But I didn't want to sleep in, not that morning. I wanted to go see Minnie and Susanna, so I could tell them all about our trip.

"Eat your breakfast first. They will be there when you get there."

Mama's cooking always tasted so good, but that day I was in such a hurry I barely noticed. I asked if I could be excused and bolted out the back door, but not before kissing Mama on the cheek and saying goodbye.

I was halfway through the yard when Mama called, "Anna, stop. I have some bread for Minnie and Susanna's family."

I thought to myself, could anything else delay my plans for the day? I ran back, took the bread from Mama, and headed off for the trees in the distance. I sprinted through the trees and climbed the hill that led to the meadow. As I ran through the wildflowers, I could see Minnie's house in the distance.

It looked different. I could see people sitting on the front porch, but I couldn't see Minnie. At first, I couldn't make out who was sitting on the porch, but as I got closer I could tell that the people on the porch were Minnie's sons and daughters. I'd never met them, but I could tell who they were by the pictures I'd seen on Minnie's mantel.

I reached the porch and asked if I could see Minnie.

"Oh, you must be Anna. Mother talked about you often," Minnie's daughter said.

I asked again if I could see Minnie as her daughter drew closer to me and placed her arm around my shoulder. I remember thinking this was odd because I didn't know her very well. She told me that Minnie had passed away the day before last.

Minnie had died while I was on my canal trip, the trip I came to tell her all about. At first the words her daughter was telling me didn't make any sense. I had come to tell her about my trip. Minnie wanted to hear all about my trip. I realized by the sad look on their faces and the quiet sobbing that Minnie was gone.

One of Minnie's daughters said, "Mother really enjoyed your visits, Anna. You brought her great joy."

I turned and started running as fast and as far as my legs would carry me. How can Minnie be gone, and why hadn't I been here when she left? I ran through the field in Minnie's backyard and kept running till I collapsed from exhaustion next to a stream.

I started crying harder than I'd ever cried before. I cried for Minnie, for her children, and for me. When I finally stopped crying, I got really mad. Mad at the canal for taking me away from Minnie when she needed me most. I picked up stones, and anything else within my reach, and threw them across the stream with all my might.

My arms started hurting from throwing the stones so hard, and I ran out of tears.

So, next I did what I had gone to Minnie's to do. I started telling Minnie about our trip on the Delaware Canal. I sat on the edge of the stream and recited my story to Minnie. I could hear her laughter in the breeze as I told her about George falling into the canal.

I'd been sitting next to the stream for what seemed like hours when I felt a gentle hand on my shoulder. I turned around and looked up to see Mama standing behind me. I stood up and Mama hugged me tighter than I'd ever been hugged before.

"Minnie's dead," I sobbed. "She died when we were away."

"I know, Anna. Minnie loved you very much, and you brought her a great deal of comfort and joy the last few years of her life. That is what you must remember when you think of Minnie. She would want that of you, Anna."

We sat on the edge of the stream and ate the bread that Mama had baked for Minnie. Mama asked if I was all right and said she was going home to the other children that she had left with Grandpa Joe.

"Do you want to come home, Anna?" she asked.

"No, I want to go see Susanna."

"Only if you're sure you're fine," she added.

Mama walked with me halfway to Susanna's house, then headed home.

As I came closer to Susanna's backyard I could see her swinging on the old swing that hung from the elm tree.

"Anna!" she shouted as she ran to greet me. We'd been friends for so long that Susanna could tell as soon as she saw me that something was wrong.

"Minnie died," I said.

"Yes, I heard. I'm sorry."

I asked if she had heard from Sam.

"No," Susanna answered.

She told me that her mother doesn't talk much anymore and keeps herself busy working around the house and taking care of her younger brother and her sisters.

Susanna talked again that afternoon in late May about her father getting a job on the "Iron Horse," now that Sam had gone off to war.

I did most of the talking as Susanna asked me questions about our trip. I told her about George falling in the canal, and about all the beautiful shops in Yardley. I told her about the bridge to Bulls Island and the excitement of being towed to the Glass House.

We talked about Minnie as we walked and ate some of the bread Mama had made for Susanna's family. When I think about the day after we returned from our trip I think about Minnie, Susanna, and Mama's homemade bread.

Chapter Thirteen
• *A Hero Returns* •

Late May turned to early June as the next week passed quickly. We had to catch up on all our chores that we missed when we were away. A great deal of work had to be done. The yard needed tending, the stable needed to be cleaned, and the vegetable garden needed to be weeded.

On the afternoon of June 3, it started raining, not just a light shower, but a persistent pattering of rain. The rain fell all afternoon, straight into the night, becoming heavy at times. The raindrops turned puddles to small pools of water, to flowing streams. We woke up the next morning and our backyard looked like a swimming hole.

I asked Mama where all the rain was coming from, and she said, "From the sky, Anna, from the sky." I knew rain fell from the sky, but the way the water was running in the streets and across the fields I figured it had to be coming from somewhere other than the sky.

Daddy and John had just left for a canal trip yesterday, and Mama started to worry about them when it was still raining after twenty-eight hours.

We went to sleep that night praying that the rain would stop. When I woke up the next morning, Mama was acting strange.

The rain had started to let up and she asked me to stay with my brothers and sister while she ran some errands. She left for town, vowing to return shortly. Mama was gone for two hours and when she returned she had a very worried look on her face.

When I asked her what was wrong, she said, "Nothing, Anna," and started preparing supper. I knew Mama, and I could tell something was wrong, so I persisted.

Mama sent Elizabeth, James, and George to their rooms and asked me to sit down. "Anna, there have been heavy rains in the Lehigh Valley north of the Blue Mountains. Many of the dams have given way and a great deal of water has swept down the Upper and Lower sections of the Lehigh Canal. Two hundred thousand to 300,000 saw logs have been carried by the current, causing much damage to the Lehigh Canal."

"What does that have to do with Daddy and John?" I asked.

"The flood has also caused damage to the Delaware Canal. There has been news of debris from the flooding reaching as far down the Delaware Canal as Riegelsville."

Mama continued, "Mr. Yoder heard that the canal is covered with lumber, houses, pig sties, and hay stacks."

"Maybe Daddy and John are past Riegelsville," I said.

"Let's pray that they are, Anna. Let's pray that they are. Don't say anything to your brothers or sister. I don't want to worry them." Mama was always thinking about everyone else.

John came running through the yard and burst through the door just as Mama was finishing her sentence.

"Where's your father?" she asked.

John answered, "He's still on the canal; he knew you'd be worried if you heard about the flood on the Lehigh, so as we came close to Smithtown, Daddy told me to run home and tell you that we're alright. There's a lot of debris in the canal, but we're going to

**Lock and dam at Lehigh Tannery,
Upper Grand Section of Lehigh Canal**

Lumber rafts are stuck on the dam. The lock was destroyed in the 1862 flood.
Pennsylvania Canal Society Collection, National Canal Museum, Easton, Pennsylvania

try to deliver our load of coal as far downstream as we can."

Just as fast as he had arrived, John was gone.

Mama and I stood there in silence wondering if we had really seen John at all.

I asked Mama if I could go over to Susanna's house to see if her father was on the canal. Mama said I could go only because the rain had stopped, but I must be very careful.

I remember running through the meadow, my feet sinking with every step I took. I started to think I was running through a bog instead of a meadow.

As I came closer to Susanna's house I could see a group of people sitting on the front porch. When I came closer to the porch I caught sight of Susanna, and she saw me. She jumped off the porch and started running toward me with a smile so broad I could see it from across her yard. I couldn't remember the last time she looked so happy.

"Anna, he's home! He's home!"

"Who's home?" I asked.

"Sam. Sam's come home."

"That's great, Susanna. You must be so excited."

"I am, Anna. Come say hello."

I couldn't see Sam; he was surrounded by family and friends. As I walked closer to the porch, the group parted, and my eyes met Sam's. His eyes looked very sad, just like Susanna's did before he came home.

I noticed the beautiful brass medal pinned to his chest. Sam extended his hand for me to shake. I took his hand and noticed that something wasn't right. My eyes gazed down to the bottom of the chair, and stopped when I didn't see two legs hanging over the chair, but only one.

I didn't know what to do, or say, so I just stared. I thought to myself, Is this why Sam has returned home? Is this why his eyes look so sad?

My silence was broken by a flurry of questions from the people standing around him. I faded into the background and started walking off the porch when Susanna stopped me and asked, "Isn't it great that Sam's home?"

"Sure," I said. "But..."

Susanna looked me right in the eye that day and said, "I know it's hard looking at his legs, and only seeing one. But, I'd rather have Sam home with one leg than not have Sam home at all."

Susanna was right of course.

Chapter Fourteen
• *Season of Change* •

When I returned home that June day in 1862, I told Mama about Sam coming home, and about his missing leg. I told her that Susanna finally looked happy again.

She said under her breath, "That blasted war! When will it end?"

We fell asleep to the sweet sound of Mama's voice singing as the wood crackled in the fireplace. All of us, except Daddy and John.

The next two days passed slowly. We were all so anxious to see Daddy and John. It had been three days since the flood of June 4, 1862, and we all went about our chores trying to keep busy.

Just as we were getting ready to sit down for dinner, the front door swung open and Daddy and John walked in, exhausted but happy to be home.

Mama ran to Daddy and threw her arms around him, and we all ran to John and embraced him.

It wasn't until we stepped back that I noticed how tired and drawn they both looked. It was if they had taken ten trips down the canal in the last five days.

Daddy and John washed up for supper and we all sat down to eat together. Mama led the family in a prayer of thanks and hope. A prayer of thanks that Daddy and John had returned home safely, that Sam had returned home safely to his family, and hope for all those who had been affected by the war and the flood. We didn't talk about the flood during supper, but talked about other things like chicken coops that needed to be fixed, and a yard that needed tending.

When supper was over, Elizabeth, James, George, and I all gave Daddy and John another hug and went up to bed.

While I lay in my bed I could hear the adults talking downstairs. I heard Daddy tell Mama that on the Lehigh Canal many people had lost their lives and many boats were destroyed. He said that a great deal of debris was flowing down the Delaware Canal. The Lehigh Navigation and Coal Company had few boats left that were not damaged, and it might take weeks for all the repairs to be completed.

Mama asked, "What will you and John do now?"

Daddy replied, "I can join one of the crews that are working to repair the canal."

John announced that it would be a good time for him to go to Easton and look for a job at the newspaper. I heard him say that he would leave the next day and send word home as soon as he was settled.

Mama asked John if he would be home to help Daddy drive the mules when the canal was repaired.

John answered, "I don't know, Mama."

I heard Daddy say, "I think it's time for Anna to drive the team, Margaret."

As I lay in bed thinking about all that I had heard that night, I realized that the next day when I woke up, everything would change. John would go to Easton, Daddy would go off to repair the Delaware Canal, and I would prepare to drive the mules.

THE END

Timeline

1832 September—Delaware Canal opens from Easton to Bristol.

1840 Outlet locks built on opposite sides of the Delaware in New Hope and Lambertville.

1841 January 8—Flood in the Lehigh Valley causes considerable damage to the Delaware Canal.

1858 Delaware Canal sold to private operators.

1862 June 4—Flood in the Lehigh Valley again causes considerable damage to the Delaware Canal.

1866 Peak Season—792,000 tons of anthracite coal were moved on the canal.

1866-1931 Delaware Canal run by the Lehigh Coal & Navigation Company.

1931   The last year of operation on the Delaware Canal.

1931   October 17—40 miles of the Delaware Canal deeded to the Commonwealth of Pennsylvania.

1940   Commonwealth of Pennsylvania acquires all 60 miles of the Delaware Canal.

1978   Delaware Canal designated as a National Historic Landmark.

Glossary

aqueduct. A structure made of steel, stone, or wood for conveying a canal over a river, creek, or hollow.

basin. A large water enclosure to one side of a canal where barges can be repaired, docked, or tied up before continuing their trip.

berm bank. The bank opposite the towpath.

bridle. A head harness for guiding a horse.

confluence. A flowing together, especially of rivers and streams.

dasher. A panel or board standing at the bow on which hung the "night-hawker."

doghouse. The housing for the mechanism of the wicket gate.

hame. Either of two curved pieces lying upon the collar in the harness to which the traces are fastened.

harness. The leather strap and metal pieces by which a horse is fastened to a vehicle.

houser. Leather covering that was placed over the horse collar.

lock. An enclosure in a canal, with a gate at each end. Used for raising or lowering boats passing from level to level.

lock tender. One who operates a lock.

night-hawker. A means of external illumination consisting of an oil lamp with polished reflector, which was placed in a boxlike structure twelve to fourteen inches on one side, enclosed by glass on three sides.

silt. Earthy matter, fine sand, or the like carried by moving water and deposited as a sediment.

snubbing post. A post around which a rope is thrown to check a boat's momentum.

tiller. A lever for turning the rudder of a barge.

tollhouse. Where boats are weighed, fees collected, and records kept.

towline. A rope tied from mules to barges for towing.

towpath. Bank of the canal where mules and drivers walk, opposite the berm bank.

trace. Either of two straps connecting a draft animal's harness to the vehicle drawn.

wicket. A small rectangular opening within the lock area, usually at the bottom of a wicket gate. It controls the flow of water when the gate is closed. A long rod extends from the top of the wicket gate to a coupling on the opening. By turning the rod a small amount of water is let through the lock; the water level reaches a depth in the lock area when the wicket is closed.

The Delaware Canal Today

The Delaware Canal is being restored and its future secured as a direct result of people and organizations working together to keep alive the history of this historical landmark.

The National Canal Museum in Easton, Pennsylvania, at the confluence of the Lehigh and Delaware Rivers, provides visitors with an appreciation of the people and places that have shaped the Delaware Canal. The museum houses reference material and offers lectures throughout the year on a variety of topics related to the Delaware Canal.

The Visitors Center in New Hope serves as the headquarters for the Friends of the Delaware Canal and offers mule-drawn boat rides. The Hugh Moore Historical Park is located in Easton, Pennsylvania, and the Delaware Canal State Park is located in Upper Black Eddy, Pennsylvania.

I would like to take this opportunity to thank Mr. Thomas Smith, Mr. Lance Metz, and the entire staff of the National Canal Museum Archives for their constant support in the pursuit of accuracy and authenticity of the information and photographs presented in this book.

Below is a list of websites that can provide more information:

http://dcnr.state.pa.us/stateparks/parks/d-canal.html

http://fodc.org

http://canals.org

Bibliography

Boardman, Fon W. Jr. *Canals.* New York: Henry Z. Walck, Inc., 1959.

Flato, Charles. *The Golden Book of the Civil War.* New York: Golden Press, 1961.

Introduction to the Friends of the Delaware Canal. (16/10/02). http://www.fodc.org/info/fodcintr.htm

McClellan, Robert J. *The Delaware Canal: A Picture Story.* New Brunswick, N.J.: Rutgers University Press, 1967.

Pennsylvania State Parks—Delaware Canal—PA DCNR. (25/9/02). http://www.dcnr.state.pa.us/stateparks/parks/d-canal.htm.

Pratt, Fletcher. *The Civil War.* Garden City, N.Y.: Doubleday & Company, Inc., 1955.

Sobol, Donald J. *A Civil War Sampler.* New York: Franklin Watts, Inc., 1961.

Yoder, C. P. "Bill." *Delaware Canal Journal.* Bethlehem, Pa.: Canal Press Incorporated, 1972.